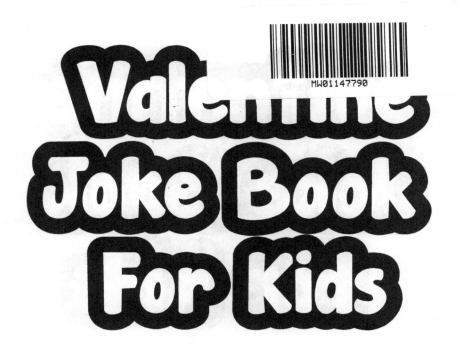

Valentine Joke Book For Kids

By: Mark Alonso

MW01147790

Valentine Joke Book For Kids

By: Mark Alonso

EMAIL US AT:
MARKALONSOBOOKS@GMAIL.COM
TO GET FREE EXTRAS!

PLEASE TITLE THE EMAIL
" *Valentine Joke Book* "
AND WE WILL SEND SOME EXTRA
SURPRISES YOUR WAY!

WHAT DO YOU CALL TWO BIRDS IN LOVE?

TWEETHEARTS!

WHAT DID THE PAPER CLIP SAY TO THE MAGNET?

I FIND YOU VERY ATTRACTIVE

WHAT DO FARMERS GIVE FOR VALENTINE'S DAY?

LOTS OF HOGS AND KISSES.

WHAT DID THE STAMP SAY TO THE ENVELOPE ON VALENTINE'S DAY?

I'M STUCK ON YOU!

WHAT DID THE WHALE SAY TO HIS
SWEETHEART ON VALENTINE'S DAY?

WHALE YOU BE MINE?

WHAT DO YOU CALL A VERY SMALL VALENTINE?

A VALEN-TINY.

WHAT DID ONE VOLCANO SAY TO THE OTHER?

I LAVA YOU.

WHAT DO OWLS SAY TO DECLARE THEIR LOVE?

OWL BE YOURS!

WHY DIDN'T THE SKELETON WANT TO SEND ANY VALENTINE'S DAY CARDS?

HIS HEART WASN'T IN IT.

WHAT DID ONE BEE SAY TO THE OTHER?

I LOVE BEE-ING WITH YOU, HONEY!

WHAT KIND OF FLOWER DO YOU NEVER GIVE ON VALENTINES DAY?

CAULIFLOWER.

WHAT HAPPENS WHEN YOU FALL IN LOVE WITH A FRENCH CHEF?

YOU GET BUTTERED UP.

DO SKUNKS CELEBRATE VALENTINE'S DAY?

SURE, THEY'RE VERY SCENT-IMENTAL!

WHY DID THE SHERIFF LOCK UP HER BOYFRIEND?

HE STOLE HER HEART.

WHAT DO YOU GET WHEN YOU KISS A DRAGON ON VALENTINE'S DAY?

THIRD DEGREE BURNS ON YOUR LIPS.

WHAT DID THE BAKER SAY TO HIS SWEETHEART?

I'M DOUGH-NUTS ABOUT YOU!

WHAT DID ONE CAT SAY TO THE OTHER CAT ON VALENTINE'S DAY?

YOU'RE PURR-FECT.

WHAT FLOWER GIVES THE MOST KISSES ON VALENTINE'S DAY?

TULIPS.

WHAT DID ONE OAR SAY TO ANOTHER?

CAN I INTEREST YOU IN A LITTLE ROW-MANCE?

WHAT DID THE SQUIRREL GIVE FOR VALENTINE'S DAY?

FORGET-ME-NUTS

WHAT DID THE CUCUMBER SAY TO THE PICKLE?

YOU MEAN A GREAT DILL TO ME.

HOW DID THE PHONE PROPOSE TO HIS GF?

HE GAVE HER A RING.

WHAT DID THE ONE SHEEP SAY TO THE OTHER?

I LOVE EWE!

AND HOW DID THE OTHER SHEEP RESPOND?

YOU'RE NOT SO BAAAAAA-D YOURSELF

WHAT DID THE TWEENAGER GIVE HIS MOM?

UGHS AND KISSES!

WHAT DID ONE LIGHT BULB SAY TO THE
OTHER LIGHT BULB ON VALENTINE'S DAY?

I WUV YOU WATTS AND WATTS!

WHAT DO YOU SAY TO AN OCTOPUS ON VALENTINE'S DAY?

I WANT TO HOLD YOUR HAND, HAND, HAND, HAND, HAND, HAND, HAND, HAND!

WHAT DO YOU CALL A GHOST'S TRUE LOVE?

HIS GHOUL-FRIEND.

WHAT DO YOU WRITE IN A SLUG'S VALENTINE'S DAY CARD?

BE MY VALEN-SLIME!

WHY IS VALENTINE'S DAY A GOOD DAY FOR A PARTY?

BECAUSE YOU CAN REALLY PARTY HEARTY!

WHAT'S THE BEST PART ABOUT VALENTINE'S DAY?

THE DAY AFTER WHEN ALL THE CANDY IS ON SALE.

WHAT DID THE PAINTER SAY TO HER SWEETHEART?

I LOVE YOU WITH ALL MY ART.

WHAT DID ROBIN HOOD SAY TO HIS GIRLFRIEND?

SHERWOOD LIKE TO BE YOUR VALENTINE.

WHY WOULD YOU WANT TO MARRY A GOALIE?

BECAUSE HE (OR SHE) IS A REAL KEEPER!

KNOCK KNOCK. WHO'S THERE?
LUKE.
LUKE WHO?
LUKE WHO GOT A VALENTINE!

KNOCK KNOCK. WHO'S THERE?
BEA.
BEA WHO?
BEA MY VALENTINE.

KNOCK KNOCK. WHO'S THERE?

AL.

AL WHO?

AL BE YOUR VALENTINE IF YOU'LL BE MINE.

KNOCK KNOCK. WHO'S THERE?

FRANK.

FRANK WHO?

FRANK YOU FOR BEING MY FRIEND!

KNOCK KNOCK.WHO'S THERE?

ARTHUR

ARTHUR WHO?

ARTHUR ANY CHOCOLATES LEFT FOR ME?

KNOCK KNOCK. WHO'S THERE?

OLIVE.

OLIVE WHO?

OLIVE YOU!

KNOCK KNOCK.WHO'S THERE?

PEAS.

PEAS WHO?

PEAS BE MY VALENTINE!

KNOCK KNOCK. WHO'S THERE?

DISGUISE.

DISGUISE WHO?

DISGUISE IS YOUR BOY FRIEND!

KNOCK KNOCK. WHO'S THERE?

BUTCH, JIMMY AND JOE.

BUTCH, JIMMY, AND JOE WHO?

BUTCH YOUR ARMS AROUND ME,
JIMMY A KISS, AND LET'S JOE.

KNOCK KNOCK. WHO'S THERE?

HOWARD.

HOWARD WHO?

HOWARD YOU LIKE A BIG KISS?

KNOCK KNOCK.WHO'S THERE?

EMMA

EMMA WHO?

EMMA HOPING I GET LOTS OF CARDS ON VALENTINE'S DAY!

KNOCK KNOCK. WHO'S THERE?

ATLAS

ATLAS WHO?

ATLAS, IT'S VALENTINE'S DAY!

KNOCK KNOCK.WHO'S THERE?

POOCH

POOCH WHO?

POOCH YOUR ARMS AROUND ME!

KNOCK KNOCK. WHO'S THERE?

SHERWOOD

SHERWOOD WHO?

SHERWOOD LIKE TO BE YOUR VALENTINE!

KNOCK KNOCK.WHO'S THERE?

ABBY.

ABBY WHO?

ABBY VALENTINE'S DAY!

KNOCK KNOCK. WHO'S THERE?

EMMA.

EMMA WHO?

EMMA HOPING I GET LOTS OF
CARDS ON VALENTINE'S DAY!

KNOCK KNOCK. WHO'S THERE?

JAMAICA.

JAMAICA WHO?

JAMAICA VALENTINE FOR ME YET?

KNOCK KNOCK. WHO'S THERE?

FRAN.

FRAN WHO?

FRANDSHIP IS A GREAT THING.

KNOCK KNOCK. WHO'S THERE?

EGG.

EGG WHO?

EGG-CITED TO BE YOUR VALENTINE.

KNOCK KNOCK. WHO'S THERE?

FONDA.

FONDA WHO?

FONDA YOU!

WHAT TYPE OF SHAPE IS MOST POPULAR ON VALENTINE'S DAY?

ACUTE TRIANGLE.

HAVE YOU GOT A DATE FOR VALENTINE'S DAY?

YEAH, IT'S FEBRUARY 14TH.

WHAT DID FRANKENSTIEN'S MONSTER SAY TO HIS BRIDE ON VALENTINE'S DAY?

BE MY VALENSTEIN!

WHAT DID ONE BLUEBERRY SAY TO THE OTHER ON VALENTINE'S DAY?

I LOVE YOU BERRY MUCH.

WHAT DID THE BOY SQUIRREL SAY TO THE GIRL SQUIRREL ON VALENTINE'S DAY?

I'M NUTS ABOUT YOU!

WHAT DID THE GIRL SQUIRREL SAY BACK TO THE BOY SQUIRREL ON VALENTINE'S DAY?

YOU'RE NUTS SO BAD YOURSELF!

WHAT DID ONE WATERMELON SAY TO THE OTHER ON VALENTINE'S DAY?

YOU'RE ONE IN A MELON!

WHERE DO ALL THE HAMBURGERS TAKE THEIR GIRLFRIENDS ON VALENTINE'S DAY?

TO A MEATBALL.

WHAT DID THE WHALE SAY TO HIS SWEETHEART ON VALENTINE'S DAY?

WHALE YOU BE MINE?

WHAT DID THE GHOST SAY TO HIS WIFE ON VALENTINE'S DAY?

YOU LOOK SO BOOTIFUL.

WHAT DID THE RABBIT SAY TO HIS GIRLFRIEND ON VALENTINE'S DAY?

SOMEBUNNY LOVES YOU!

WHAT DID THE CALCULATOR SAY TO THE PENCIL ON VALENTINE'S DAY?

YOU CAN ALWAYS COUNT ON ME.

WHAT DID THE DRUM SAY TO THE OTHER DRUM ON VALENTINE'S DAY?

MY HEART BEATS FOR YOU.

WHAT DO ELEPHANTS SAY TO ONE ANOTHER ON VALENTINE'S DAY?

I LOVE YOU A TON.

WHAT DID ONE MONSTER SAY TO THE OTHER MONSTER?

A)

BE MY VALEN-SLIME!

Q)

WHAT DID THE BOY PICKLE SAY TO THE GIRL PICKLE?

YOU MEAN A GREAT DILL TO ME.

WHAT IS IT CALLED WHEN FISH FALL IN LOVE?

GUPPY-LOVE

WHY DID THE BOY PUT CANDY UNDER HIS PILLOW?

BECAUSE HE WANTED SWEET DREAMS!

DID YOU HEAR ABOUT THE PORCUPINE WHO LOST HIS GLASSES?

HE FELL IN LOVE WITH A PINCUSHION!

WHAT'S THE PERFECT THING TO SAY TO A COFFEE-LOVER ON VALENTINE'S DAY?

WORDS CANNOT ESPRESSO WHAT YOU MEAN TO ME.

DID ADAM AND EVE EVER HAVE A DATE?

NO, THEY HAD AN APPLE!

WHY DID THE FROG CROSS THE ROAD?

BECAUSE HE WANTED TO SHOW HIS GIRLFRIEND HE HAD GUTS.

WHAT HAPPENED TO THE BED BUGS WHO FELL IN LOVE?

THEY GOT MARRIED IN THE SPRING.

WHAT DO GHOSTS SAY TO ONE ANOTHER TO SHOW THAT THEY CARE?

I LOVE BOO!

WHY DID THE ROOSTER CROSS THE ROAD?

HE WANTED TO IMPRESS THE CHICKS!

WHY DID THE CHICKEN CROSS THE ROAD?

BECAUSE HER BOYFRIEND WAS ON THE OTHER SIDE.

WHO DID DRACULA TAKE TO THE MOVIES?

HIS GHOUL FRIEND.

WHAT DO BUNNIES DO WHEN THEY GET MARRIED?

GO ON A BUNNYMOON!

WHY DID THE ROOSTER GET A TATTOO?

HE WANTED TO IMPRESS THE CHICKS!

WHAT DID THE GHOST SAY TO HIS WIFE?

YOU LOOK SO BOOTIFUL.

WHO DID DRACULA BRING TO THE PROM?

A)

HIS GHOUL FRIEND.

WHAT KIND OF GIRL DOES A MUMMY TAKE ON A DATE?

A)

ANY OLD GIRL HE CAN DIG UP.

WHAT SOUND DO PORCUPINES MAKE WHEN THEY KISS?

OUCHY, MAMA!

WHAT DID THE SNAKE SAY TO HIS GIRLFRIEND ON VALENTINE'S DAY?

GIVE ME A LITTLE HISS.

WHY DO VALENTINE'S HAVE HEARTS ON THEM?

BECAUSE BRAINS WOULD BE PRETTY GROSS!

WHAT DID THE BAT SAY TO HIS GIRLFRIEND?

YOU'RE FUN TO HANG AROUND WITH.

HOW DOES CUPID VISIT HIS GIRLFRIEND?

ON AN ARROW-PLANE!

WHY ARE ANGEL MARRIAGES SO GOOD?

BECAUSE THEY LIVE HARP-ILY EVER AFTER.

WHY DID THE BOY SEND HIS GIRLFRIEND'S VALENTINE THROUGH TWITTER?

BECAUSE SHE WAS HIS TWEETHEART.

WHAT DO YOU GET WHEN YOU CROSS A DOG WITH A VALENTINE CARD?

A CARD THAT SAYS, "I LOVE YOU DROOL-LY"!

KNOCK KNOCK.WHO'S THERE?

HAL.

HAL WHO?

HAL ABOUT BEING MY VALENTINE?

KNOCK KNOCK. WHO'S THERE?

HEYWOOD.

HEYWOOD WHO?

HEYWOOD YOU BE MY VALENTINE?

KNOCK KNOCK. WHO'S THERE?

IRIS.

IRIS WHO?

IRIS YOU WERE HERE.

KNOCK KNOCK. WHO'S THERE?

IGUANA

IGUANA WHO?

IGUANA HOLD YOUR HAND.

KNOCK KNOCK.WHO'S THERE?

POOCH.

POOCH WHO?

POOCH YOUR ARMS AROUND ME.

KNOCK KNOCK. WHO'S THERE?

HONEYDEW.

HONEYDEW WHO?

HONEYDEW YOU WANT TO BE MY
VALENTINE?

KNOCK KNOCK.WHO'S THERE?

JIMMY.

JIMMY WHO?

JIMMY A LITTLE KISS.

KNOCK KNOCK. WHO'S THERE?

ZOO.

ZOO WHO?

ZOO WANT TO BE MY VALENTINE?

KNOCK KNOCK.WHO'S THERE?
LOVES.
LOVES WHO?
LOVES YOU!

KNOCK KNOCK. WHO'S THERE?
EYESORE.
EYESORE WHO?
EYESORE DO LIKE YOU!

KNOCK KNOCK.WHO'S THERE?

ORANGE.

ORANGE WHO?

ORANGE YOU GLAD IT'S VALENTINE'S DAY?

KNOCK KNOCK. WHO'S THERE?

WILL.

WILL WHO?

WILL YOU BE MY VALENTINE?!

KNOCK KNOCK.WHO'S THERE?

FANGS.

FANGS WHO?

FANGS FOR BEING MY VALENTINE.

KNOCK KNOCK. WHO'S THERE?

IVAN.

IVAN WHO?

IVAN TO BE YOUR VALENTINE.

WHY IS LETTUCE THE MOST LOVING VEGETABLE?

BECAUSE ITS GOT HEART.

HOW MUCH CANDY DO YOU HOPE TO GET THIS VALENTINE'S DAY?

A CHOCO-LOT!

WHAT'S THE MOST ROMANTIC PART OF A FORK?

ITS VALEN-TINES.

WHAT'S CUPID'S FAVORITE SUPERHERO TV SHOW?

ARROW.

WHAT HAPPENED WHEN THE TWO ANGELS GOT MARRIED?

THEY LIVED HARPILY EVER AFTER.

WHY DID THE BANANA GO OUT WITH THE PRUNE?

BECAUSE IT COULDN'T GET A DATE.

WHAT DID THE BOY BIRD SAY TO THE GIRL BIRD ON VALENTINE'S DAY?

LET ME CALL YOU TWEET HEART!

WHAT DID THE LIGHT BULB SAY TO THE SWITCH?

YOU TURN ME ON.

WHAT IS A RAM'S FAVORITE SONG ON FEBRUARY 14TH?

I ONLY HAVE EYES FOR EWE, DEAR.

IF YOUR AUNT RAN OFF TO GET MARRIED, WHAT WOULD YOU CALL HER?

A)

ANTELOPE.

WHAT DID THE CHOCOLATE SYRUP SAY TO THE ICE CREAM?

I'M SWEET ON YOU!

DID YOU HEAR ABOUT THE NEARSIGHTED PORCUPINE?

HE FELL IN LOVE WITH A PIN CUSHION!

WHAT'S THE DIFFERENCE BETWEEN A $20 STEAK AND A $55 STEAK?

FEBRUARY 14TH.

WHAT DID ONE MUSHROOM SAY TO THE OTHER ON VALENTINE'S DAY?

THERE'S SO MUSHROOM IN MY HEART FOR YOU!

WHAT DID ONE BEET SAY TO THE OTHER ON VALENTINE'S DAY?

YOU MAKE MY HEART BEET FASTER!

WHAT DID ONE MUFFIN SAY TO THE OTHER ON VALENTINE'S DAY?

YOU'RE MY STUD-MUFFIN!

WHAT DID THE TOAST SAY TO THE BUTTER ON VALENTINE'S DAY?

YOU'RE MY BUTTER HALF!

WHY DOES CUPID ALWAYS MAKE SO MUCH MONEY AT THE CASINO?

BECAUSE HE'S A VALENTINE'S CARD SHARK.

WHY SHOULDN'T YOU FALL IN LOVE WITH A PASTRY CHEF?

HE'LL DESSERT YOU.

WHAT IS THE MOST ROMANTIC CITY IN ENGLAND?

LOVERPOOL.

WHAT DID THE DRUM SAY TO THE OTHER DRUM ON VALENTINE'S DAY?

MY HEART BEATS FOR YOU.

WHAT DID CAVEMEN GIVE THEIR WIVES ON VALENTINE'S DAY?

LOTS OF UGHS AND KISSES.

WHAT DO SINGLE PEOPLE CALL VALENTINE'S DAY?

HAPPY INDEPENDENCE DAY

WHAT DID THE PAINTER SAY TO HER BOYFRIEND?

I LOVE YOU WITH ALL MY ART!

WHY DID THE GOD OF LOVE BECOME A
BLACKJACK DEALER?

BECAUSE HE WAS ALWAYS GREAT AT THE
CUPID SHUFFLE.

WHAT WAS THE THUNDER CLOUD'S FAVORITE
GIFT TO GIVE ON VALENTINE'S DAY?

A BOX OF SHOCKLATES.

WHY SHOULD YOU NEVER BREAKUP WITH A GOALIE?

BECAUSE HE'S A KEEPER.

WHAT DID ONE BOAT SAY TO THE OTHER?

ARE YOU UP FOR A LITTLE ROW-MANCE?

WHAT DID THE GUY WITH THE BROKEN LEG SAY TO HIS NURSE?

I'VE GOT A CRUTCH ON YOU.

HOW CAN YOU TELL THE CALENDAR IS POPULAR?

BECAUSE YOU CAN PARTY HEARTY.

WHAT DO YOU CALL ROMANCE IN TROPICAL FISH TANK?

GUPPY LOVE.

WHY DID THE BOY PUT CLOTHES ON THE VALENTINES HE WAS SENDING?

BECAUSE THEY NEEDED TO BE AD-DRESSED.

WHAT DID THE LIGHT BULB SAY TO THE SWITCH?

YOU TURN ME ON.

WHAT DID PILGRIMS GIVE EACH OTHER ON VALENTINE'S DAY?

MAYFLOWERS

WHAT DID ONE FONT SAY TO THE OTHER ON VALENTINE'S DAY?

YOU'RE JUST MY TYPE.

WHAT FOOD IS CRAZY ABOUT VALENTINE'S DAY CHOCOLATES?

A COCOA-NUT.

WHAT WAS THE FRENCH CAT'S FAVORITE VALENTINE'S DAY DESSERT?

CHOCOLATE MOUSSE

WHAT DID THE SEAMSTRESS SAY TO EXPRESS HER LOVE?

YOU'RE SEW SPECIAL TO ME.

WHICH ANIMAL SHARES THE MOST LOVE?

A HEARTVAARK

WHAT DO YOU GET WHEN YOU CROSS A DOG WITH A VALENTINE CARD?

A CARD THAT SAYS "I LOVE YOU DROOL-LY"

WHAT DOES SOMEONE WHO LOVES THEIR CAR DO ON FEBRUARY 14?

THEY GIVE IT A VALENSHINE.

DID YOU HEAR ABOUT THE MAN WHO PROMISED HIS GIRLFRIEND A DIAMOND FOR VALENTINE'S DAY?

A)

HE TOOK HER TO A BASEBALL PARK.

WHAT DID THE BOY SHEEP SAY TO THE GIRL SHEEP ON VALENTINE'S DAY?

YOU'RE NOT SO BAAAA-D.

WHAT DOES A CARPET SALESMAN GIVE HIS WIFE FOR VALENTINE'S DAY?

RUGS AND KISSES.

WHAT IS A RAM'S FAVORITE SONG ON FEBRUARY 14TH?

I ONLY HAVE EYES FOR EWE, DEAR.

WHAT HAPPENED WHEN THE TWO TENNIS PLAYERS MET?

IT WAS LOB AT FIRST SIGHT.

WHAT DID ONE DOOR BELL SAY TO THE OTHER ON FEBRUARY 14TH?

BE MY VALENCHIME.

WHAT DID THE WHIPPED CREAM SAY TO THE ICE CREAM ON VALENTINE'S DAY?

I'M SWEET ON YOU.

WHY DID THE BANANA GO OUT WITH THE PRUNE?

BECAUSE IT COULDN'T GET A DATE.

WHY DID THE PIG GIVE HIS GIRLFRIEND A BOX OF CANDY?

IT WAS VALENSWINE'S DAY.

WHY ARE ARTICHOKES THE MOST LOVING VEGETABLE?

BECAUSE THEY HAVE HEART.

WHAT IS CUPID'S FAVORITE ROCK BAND?

HEART

WHAT WAS THE THUNDER CLOUD'S FAVORITE GIFT TO GIVE ON VALENTINE'S DAY?

A BOX OF SHOCKLATES.

DID YOU HEAR ABOUT THE NEARSIGHTED PORCUPINE?

HE FELL IN LOVE WITH A PIN CUSHION!

BONUS

HILARIOUS JOKES FOR KIDS

&

BEST RIDDLES FOR KIDS THAT
WON'T BE TOO HARD TO SOLVE

WHAT DO YOU CALL A DINOSAUR THAT IS SLEEPING?

A DINO-SNORE!

WHAT IS FAST, LOUD AND CRUNCHY?

A ROCKET CHIP!

WHY DID THE TEDDY BEAR SAY NO TO DESSERT?

BECAUSE SHE WAS STUFFED.

WHAT HAS EARS BUT CANNOT HEAR?

A CORNFIELD.

WHAT DID THE LEFT EYE SAY TO THE RIGHT EYE?

BETWEEN US, SOMETHING SMELLS!

WHAT DID ONE PLATE SAY TO THE OTHER PLATE?

DINNER IS ON ME!

WHY DID THE STUDENT EAT HIS HOMEWORK?

BECAUSE THE TEACHER TOLD HIM IT WAS A PIECE OF CAKE!

WHAT IS BROWN, HAIRY AND WEARS SUNGLASSES?

A COCONUT ON VACATION.

WHY WAS 6 AFRAID OF 7?

BECAUSE 7, 8, 9

WHEN DOES A JOKE BECOME A "DAD" JOKE?

WHEN THE PUNCHLINE IS A PARENT.

WHAT GETS CRACKED BEFORE YOU USE IT?

AN EGG.

WHAT BEGINS WITH AN "E" BUT ONLY HAS ONE LETTER?

AN ENVELOPE.

WHAT HAS WORDS BUT NEVER SPEAKS?

A BOOK!

WHAT GOES UP BUT NEVER COMES BACK DOWN?

YOUR AGE!

WHERE DO COWS GO FOR ENTERTAINMENT?

THE MOO-VIES.

WHY ARE GHOSTS SUCH BAD LIARS?

YOU CAN SEE RIGHT THOUGH THEM.

WHAT DO YOU CALL A SAD STRAWBERRY?

A BLUEBERRY.

WHERE DO YOU FIND KEYS THAT WON'T WORK IN A LOCK?

ON A PIANO.

WHY COULDN'T THE MOON FINISH HIS MEAL?

HE WAS FULL!

WHAT ROOM DOESN'T HAVE ANY WINDOWS?

MUSHROOM.

HOW DO YOU TALK TO A GIANT?

USE BIG WORDS!

WHAT FALLS IN WINTER BUT NEVER GETS HURT?

SNOW!

WHY WAS THE BABY STRAWBERRY CRYING?

BECAUSE HER PARENTS WERE IN A JAM.

WHAT DID THE LITTLE CORN SAY TO THE MAMA CORN?

WHERE IS POP CORN?

WHAT DID THE BANANA SAY TO THE DOG?

NOTHING. BANANAS CAN'T TALK.

WHY DID THE DINOSAUR CROSS THE ROAD?

BECAUSE THE CHICKEN WASN'T BORN YET.

WHAT DID THE NOSE SAY TO THE FINGER?

QUIT PICKING ON ME!

WHAT DO ELVES LEARN IN SCHOOL?

THE ELF-ABET.